CONTENTS

BIG DOGS
are
LAP DOGS
too

BIG DOGS love to nestle and nuzzle...

and cuddle…

...and kiss.

They have favorite stuffed toys…

…and some wear fashionable sweaters.

BIG DOGS are tender and kind
to small children...

and will protect them
from any harm...

...and be playful and patient with a child's whims.

Big dogs LIKE little kittens and little pugs…

...and they especially like GREAT BIG hugs!

Big dog puppies LOVE to sit on laps …

and once grown, a lap is still a big dog's favorite place to be...

...even when they are BIGGER than the laps they are trying to sit on!

The NATURE of BIG DOGS

BIG DOGS have big hair...

and big smiles...

big tongues...

and big drool.

BIG bad
breath…

and the
BIGGEST hearts.

BIG DOGS
have big
paws...

and big tails that make big wags.

They have big appetites...

and big
thirsts.

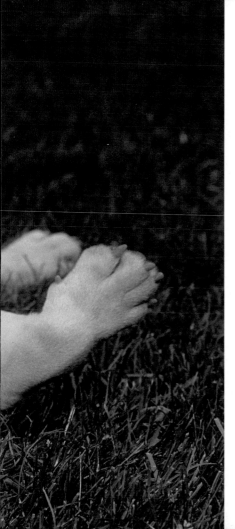

They live in a state of
BIG BLISS...

and offer
BIG LOVE to
anybody who
will take it.

BIG DOGS give
big kisses...

...and warm the WHOLE bed (not just the pillow).

BIG DOGS have big energy...

and greet
their owners
with big
enthusiasm.

They make BIG splashes…

...and have BIG fun.

They perform big tasks and offer BIG help…

...and allow us to go on BIG adventures.

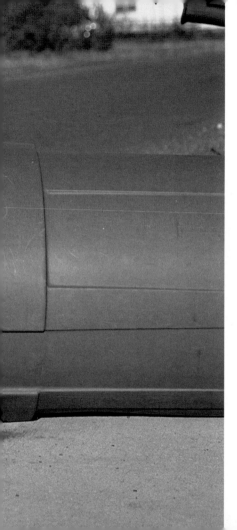

BIG DOGS also make
big messes...

and get into
big trouble…

and even have some rather big attitude…

but big dog owners don't mind...

...because nothing beats having
a BIG DOG in your lap!

BIG DOG
FACTS
& FUN

The most popular dog in America is the Labrador Retriever, a GREAT big dog! The second and third most popular dogs are the Golden Retriever and the German Shepherd respectively... two more GREAT big dogs.

THE BIGGEST BIG DOGS

Mastiff (175-190 lbs.; 27-30" tall)
St. Bernard (120-200 lbs.; 25-28" tall)
Great Swiss Mountain Dog (135 lbs.; 23-28" tall)
Newfoundland (110-150 lbs.; 26-28" tall)
Great Dane (100-120 lbs.; 28-30+" tall)
Irish Wolfhound (105-120 lbs.; 30-35" tall)
Bullmastiff (100-130 lbs.; 25-27" tall)
Great Pyrenees (90-130 lbs.; 26-32" tall)
Komondor (80-135 lbs.; 26-35" tall)
Bernese Mountain Dog (80-120 lbs.; 23-27" tall)
Portuguese Watchdog (95-110 lbs.; 30" tall)
Alaskan Malamute (85-125 lbs.; 23-28" tall)
Rottweiler (90-110 lbs.; 23-27" tall)
Akita (75-110 lbs.; 24-28" tall)
Bloodhound (80-110 lbs.; 23-27" tall)

Almost all of the BIG DOGS were originally working dogs, known for their intelligence and hardiness. The large and lovable ST. BERNARD (above) was first used for draft work during the Middle Ages. The massive, water-loving NEWFOUNDLAND (opposite) was used in cod fisheries to pull nets and boats ashore.

The giant and gentle GREAT DANE is not Danish but German, and known as the Deutsche Dogge in its native land. Its ancestors were used as war dogs and hunting dogs, but today, this great big dog is a loving, easy-going, elegant, and LARGE family pet.

Present in Ireland almost 2,000 years ago, the enormous IRISH WOLFHOUND was originally used to hunt wolves. It is the tallest of all the sighthounds, and resembles a bulky, powerful, rough-coated greyhound.

Another ancient, BIG breed, the BERNESE MOUNTAIN DOG is the
most popular of the Swiss mountain dogs. This strong, tough
canine originally served as a draft dog.

The big and strong ALASKAN MALAMUTE is named after the Mahlemut Inuit living on the arctic coast of western Alaska. These hardy dogs would originally accompany seal and polar bear hunters and haul the heavy carcasses home.

One of the most useful breeds to humans, the incredible
BLOODHOUND is an ancient scent-tracker that has been used to
hunt animals, criminals, and lost children.

SMALLER BIG DOGS

German Shepherd (75-95 lbs.; 22-26" tall)
Doberman Pinscher (65-90 lbs.; 24-28" tall)
Giant Schnauzer (65-90 lbs.; 24-28" tall)
Borzoi (60-105 lbs.; 26-28" tall)
Weimaraner (70-85 lbs.; 22-27" tall)
Rhodesian Ridgeback (65-85 lbs.; 24-27" tall)
Old English Sheep Dog (60-90 lbs.; 22-24" tall)
Boxer (55-80 lbs.; 21-25" tall)
Golden Retriever (60-80 lbs.; 20-24" tall)
Labrador Retriever (55-80 lbs.; 21-23" tall)
Greyhound (60-70 lbs.; 27-30" tall)
German Pointers (60-70 lbs.; 24-26" tall)
Bulldog (50-55 lbs.; 12-14" tall)
Bearded Collie (40-60 lbs.; 20-22" tall)

In the late 1800s, Louis Dobermann of Germany used the Rottweiler, German Pinscher, Weimaraner, English Greyhound, and Manchester Terrier to develop the resourceful and intelligent DOBERMAN PINSCHER. Today, Dobermans are companion and service dogs all over the world.

The lean and speedy BORZOI (also known as the Russian Wolfhound) was popular with the Russian aristocracy for hunting wolves. Borzoi is the Russian word for sighthound.

The uniquely-colored WEIMARANER (opposite) is a versatile hunting dog from Germany, while the muscular RHODESIAN RIDGEBACK (above) was developed in Africa to trail big game, such as lions, which led to its other name, "African Lion Hound."

The jolly and gentle OLD ENGLISH SHEEPDOG (below) was used to defend flocks and herds, and to drive cattle and sheep to market. The playful and exuberant BOXER (opposite) was developed in Germany in the late 1800s, and was one of the first breeds to be employed as a police and military dog.

The affable, athletic, eager-to-please GOLDEN RETRIEVER (above) and LABRADOR RETRIEVER (opposite) are the two most popular dog breeds in America. Excellent retrievers of downed waterfowl and upland birds, these dogs also make wonderful family pets.

The extremely fast GREYHOUND (it can reach 37 mph) has been called "the world's fastest couch potato," because of its quiet and calm nature. An extremely old breed, Greyhound-like dogs are seen in artwork from ancient Egyptian, Greek, and Roman times.

The agile, handsome, and obedient GERMAN SHORT-HAIRED POINTER was developed to be an extremely versatile hunting dog, combining pointing, retrieving, and trailing skills.

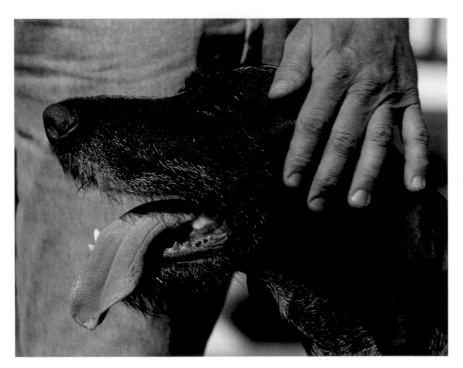

The GERMAN WIRE-HAIRED POINTER is a combination of the French Griffon, Pudelpointer, Short-haired Pointer, and Broken-coated Pointer. It was developed to be an all-purpose, water and land-working pointer and retriever.

The COLLIE'S original function was herding sheep in the cold regions of northern Scotland. It is still an active, strong dog that can change speed and direction instantly, as required in herding.

The high-spirited, boisterous BEARDED COLLIE is a tireless herder of sheep and drover of cattle, which means it also plays tirelessly and requires lots of vigorous activity.

The SALUKI (left) is a sighthound and is perhaps the most ancient breed of domestic dog. Arab nomads used Salukis to run down gazelles, foxes, and hares in the desert. The BERGAMASCO (opposite) is also an ancient breed that was first used for livestock guarding. Its unique corded coat evolved to protect it from the weather and from the flailing hooves of livestock.

The BORDER COLLIE (opposite) is still the most popular working sheepdog in Great Britain and Ireland, and is among the most intelligent and obedient of breeds. The AFGHAN (below) is another ancient sighthound. Generations of hunting in the harsh mountains of Afghanistan produced a fast, nimble, and strong dog.